Also available in this series from Quadrille:

MINDFULNESS
MINDFULNESS II
QUIET
FRIENDSHIP
LOVE
CONFIDENCE
TIDINESS
HAPPINESS
MOTHERHOOD
LUCK
US
SEX

the little book of

CHRISTMAS

Hardie Grant

QUADRILLE

Christmas

Definition:
noun

1. Church festival observed annually in memory of the birth of Christ.

2. Derived from the Old English *Cristes maesse* from Christ and mass. First used as one word from the mid-14th century.

That Christmas is still celebrated 2,000 years after Jesus's birth is down to the astonishing idea that God had become man in the form of a tiny vulnerable baby.

Christmas, and a new era, was born.

The Birth of Baby Jesus

Christmas began with the birth of a baby in Bethlehem 2,000 years ago. Most modern historians place Jesus's birth sometime around AD4.

Try to imagine whizzing back in time, to the era of the Roman Empire: a place of slavery, crucifixions, of gladiators and animal sacrifice. Into this violent world, a tiny baby is born and is tenderly cradled by his young, unmarried mother.

This loving, all too human image presented a new example of godliness to the world.

"For unto us a child is born,
To us a son is given;
And the government shall be
upon his shoulder;
And his name shall be called
Wonderful, Counsellor, Mighty God,
Everlasting Father, Prince of Peace."

ISAIAH
Chapter 9, Verse 6

"And she brought forth her firstborn son, and wrapped him in swaddling clothes and laid him in a manger; because there was no room for them in the inn."

LUKE
Chapter 2, Verse 7

Who Is Joseph?

First referenced in the gospels of Luke and Matthew, St. Joseph was the earthly father of Jesus Christ and the husband of the Virgin Mary.

Who Is Mary?

Mary, the mother of Jesus Christ, is known by many names, including Blessed Virgin Mary, Our Lady and Queen of Heaven.

In the West Country of England, legend holds that at midnight on Christmas Eve animals in barns or stalls all kneel down in homage to the birth of Jesus.

"We pictured the meek mild
creatures where
They dwelt in their strawy pen,
Nor did it occur to one of us there
To doubt they were kneeling then."

THOMAS HARDY

From *The Oxen*

Robin Redbreast

Storytellers report that soon after Jesus was born, the Holy Family made a fire to keep warm. When it began to fade, Mary asked the nearby animals if they could help.

A nondescript brown bird started flapping its wings to revive the fire and it was soon flaming hot. After a spark caught the bird on its chest, Mary announced that thereafter the robin would always have a red breast.

Of all the characters in the nativity story, angels are the most numerous. They visit the as yet unmarried Mary and Joseph to explain quite how she fell pregnant. After the birth, an angel, and then the 'heavenly host', visit the shepherds, to tell of the good news.

Placing angels on the top of Christmas trees today is a reminder of their presence during the nativity.

"And suddenly there was with the angel a multitude of the heavenly host praising God and saying, Glory be to God in the highest, and on earth peace, good will toward men."

LUKE
Chapter 2, Verses 13–14

Baby's First Visitors: The Shepherds

No, not that nice family from next door, but actual live shepherds fresh from the hills... God's way of showing his softer side and reaching out to the laymen.

"What can I give Him,
Poor as I am?
If I were a Shepherd
I would bring a lamb;
If I were a Wise Man
I would do my part,
Yet what I can I give Him,
Give my heart."

CHRISTINA ROSSETTI
From 'In the Bleak Midwinter'

"We three kings of Orient are,
Bearing gifts we traverse afar
Field and fountain, moor and mountain
Following yonder star

O Star of wonder, star of night
Star with royal beauty bright
Westward leading, still proceeding
Guide us to thy Perfect Light."

JOHN HENRY HOPKINS JR.
From 'We Three Kings'

What Could the Star of Bethlehem Have Been?

- A comet
- A conjunction between Jupiter and Saturn
- A supernova

"And when they were come into the house, they saw the young child with Mary his mother, and fell down, and worshipped him: and when they had opened their treasures, they presented unto him gifts; gold, and frankincense and myrrh."

MATTHEW
Chapter 2, Verse 11

Names of the Three Wise Men

Gaspar, Melchior and Balthazar (Western Christianity)

Larvandad, Gushnasaph and Hormisdas (Syrian Christianity)

Hor, Karsudan and Basanater (Ethiopian Christianity)

Kagpha, Badadakharida and Badadilma (Armenian Catholicism)

Forget Prosecco and teeny-weeny baby hats, Mary enjoyed the blingiest baby shower ever, thanks to the gold, frankincense and myrrh given by wise men from the East.

The Gifts

Gold is associated with royalty and is seen as a symbol of kingship on earth.

Frankincense creates a strong and beautiful aroma; it is sometimes used in worship in churches and is associated with divine status.

Myrrh is a fragrant spice that is used as an embalming oil; Christians believe that it showed that Jesus would die.

"Behold, the angel of the Lord appeared to Joseph in a dream, saying, Arise, and take the young child and his mother, and flee into Egypt."

Baby Jesus as a Refugee

Fearing that a wrathful King Herod wanted to kill any child who claimed kingship, Mary, Joseph and Jesus left Bethlehem and travelled to Egypt, only returning to Israel after Herod's death.

An old sycamore tree in the El Matareya district of Cairo is still venerated by Christian pilgrims as a place where the Holy Family took shelter during their time as refugees.

According to mythology, a spider spun a web over the cave's entrance where the Holy Family were hiding from Herod's soldiers. Spider web decorations are popular today in the Ukraine.

Who Was Born on Christmas Day?

1642 Sir Isaac Newton, physicist

1821 Clara Barton, founder of the
American Red Cross

1899 Humphrey Bogart, actor

1949 Sissy Spacek, actress

1954 Annie Lennox, singer

1971 Justin Trudeau, Prime Minister
of Canada

Christmas Around the World

English: Happy Christmas

Finnish: *Hyvää Joulua*

French: *Joyeux Noël*

German: *Frohe Weihnachten*

Icelandic: *Gleðileg Jól*

Italian: *Buon Natale*

Romanian: *Craciun Fericit*

Polish: *Wesołych Świąt*

Portuguese: *Feliz Natal*

Spanish: *Feliz Navidad*

Swedish: *God Jul*

Bees, all over the world, have been reported to buzz Christmas tunes at midnight on Christmas Eve. In Missouri they are said to hum the Old Hundredth Psalm.

According to Regional Folklore, Which Animals Pull the Christmas Gift-Giver's Sleigh?

- Sweden: Goats
- Australia: White kangaroos
- Netherlands: White horse
- Russia: Foals

Some Worldwide Centrepieces for the Main Christmas Feast

- Costa Rica: Tamales

- Greece: Lamb

- Iceland: Smoked lamb

- Jamaica: Curried goat

- Japan: Fried chicken

- Norway: Mutton ribs

- Portugal: Cod

- Romania: Gammon

- Russia: Pork

- Poland: Carp

- Puerto Rico: Suckling pig

Orthodox Christians follow the Julian, rather than the western Gregorian calendar, which means that in Russia and other orthodox countries, Christmas falls on 7 January, as the two calendars are 13 days apart.

On 6 January, Orthodox Christmas Eve, Christians traditionally fast until the appearance of the first star in the night sky, symbolizing the birth of Christ.

South America

All over South America, Christmas Eve is celebrated by attending midnight mass, explosive firework displays, late suppers and family parties that can go on until the early hours of the morning. As a result, Christmas Day is an altogether quieter affair.

Australia

There is more to an Australian Christmas than BBQs on the beach (although they are certainly very popular).

Blazing sunshine and clowns join together in Australia's Adelaide Christmas Pageant. Established in 1933, the parade attracts hundreds of thousands of spectators who cheer the procession of floats, entertainers and finally the arrival of Father Christmas.

America

America has contributed many things to the Christmas story including:

- Elves: though elves do play a large, mischievous part in European folklore, we have Americans to thank for attaching them to Santa. Elves were first mentioned in *Christmas Elves*, by Louisa M. Alcott in 1856.

- *Twas the Night Before Christmas*: a delightful poem originally published in 1823 as *A Visit from St. Nicholas* by Clement Clarke Moore.

- Best Christmas songs: from favourite carols 'O Little Town of Bethlehem'

(Phillips Brooks) to 'We Three Kings of Orient Are' (John Henry Hopkins Jr) and songs, 'Santa Claus is Comin' to Town' (John Frederick Coots) and 'Jingle Bells' (James Pierpont), Americans have written the soundtrack to Christmas.

- *It's a Wonderful Life:* consistently voted the favourite Christmas film, starring James Stewart and Donna Reed, and directed by Frank Capra in 1946.

- Coca-Cola Christmas trucks: first used in an advertising campaign in 1995, a real Coca-Cola Christmas truck appeared in America in 2001.

Austria

Germany's most iconic carol, 'Stille Nacht' was written by Franz Xaver Gruber to lyrics by Joseph Mohr in Austria in 1818.

UNESCO declared the carol to be of 'intangible cultural heritage' in 2011.

Stille Nacht, heilige Nacht,
Alles schläft; einsam wacht
Nur das traute hochheilige Paar.
Holder Knabe im lockigen Haar,
Schlaf in himmlischer Ruh!
Schlaf in himmlischer Ruh!

Silent night, holy night,
All is calm, all is bright
Round yon virgin mother and child.
Holy infant, so tender and mild,
Sleep in heavenly peace,
Sleep in heavenly peace.

Bulgaria

Made with no yeast or eggs, Bulgarian Christmas Eve bread, *pitka*, comprises a piece for each family member and an extra for the house.

Within one piece, a silver coin is baked, and whoever chooses the piece of bread will enjoy fortune for the following year.

China

With only one per cent of China's population officially Christian, Christmas is not generally celebrated. However, Christmas apples are sometimes given with messages such as 'peace' or 'love' printed on them.

Croatia

The four candles on the Croatian advent wreath represent:

- Creation of the world
- Embodiment of Christ
- Redemption on the cross
- End of all things

Ethiopia

Ethiopian legend suggests that after hearing the news of Jesus's birth, the shepherds began celebrating with their staffs by playing a game not unlike hockey.

This game, known as *genna*, is played by Ethiopian young men on Christmas Day.

Finland

Christmas Eve in Finland sees as many as 75 per cent of the population visit graveyards and cemeteries to light candles and honour their ancestors. The tranquil candlelit scene in the winter darkness is a magically moving sight.

Georgia

The *chichilaki* is a Georgian Christmas tree made from the curly white shavings of dried walnut and hazelnut branches. Decorated with fruits and berries, *chichilaki's* white 'leaves' are said to resemble the beard of St. Basil the Great.

Germany

There is simply nothing like an authentic German Christmas market, *Christkindlmarkt* or *Weihnachtsmärkte*, in which to imbibe that intangible Christmassy feeling.

Christmas markets, whether in Nuremberg or Berlin, or Birmingham or Lincoln, sell not only wooden toys, *glühwein* and *bratwurst*, but also romance, sparkle, and Christmas warmth.

Over 40 *Weihnachtsmärkte* take place every Christmas time in Germany, and hundreds more the world over.

Founded in 1434, Striezelmarkt, Dresden's Christmas market is the oldest in Germany. With over 200 stands, its Christmas cheer attracts three million visitors a year.

Delicious Christmas Treats from Germany

- *Eierlikör*: alcoholic punch, similar to eggnog
- Gingerbread house: gingerbread, iced and decorated with sweets
- *Glühwein / Gløgg*: mulled wine
- *Lebkuchen*: festive ginger biscuits
- Stollen: fruit bread stuffed with fruit and marzipan

Greece

Karavaki: traditional Greek Christmas decorated boats.

As a seafaring nation Greece has always honoured St. Nicholas, patron saint of sailors, and recently Greeks have been reviving the old custom of decorating sailing boats with Christmas lights.

In 2013, Athens took up the new (old) tradition by erecting a *karavaki* in Syntagma Square, in front of the Greek parliament building.

Iceland

Iceland wins the award for coolest Christmas thanks to their Yule Lads. Thirteen trolls, the offspring of two giants, Gryla and Leppalúði, descend from the mountains during the Christmas period and cause pranks and chaos. They have also been reported to leave small gifts in children's shoes.

Icelandic folklore holds that at midnight on Christmas Eve, the animals begin talking for an hour. Only the godly can hear what they have to say.

The 13 Icelandic Yule Lads

1. Stekkjarstaur
2. Giljagaur
3. Stúfur
4. Þvörusleikir
5. Pottaskefill
6. Askasleikir

Japan

Until the 1970s, Japan had no history of celebrating Christmas. However, thanks to a clever fast-food marketing campaign, it has become a Christmas tradition to enjoy a Kentucky Fried Chicken Christmas Day takeaway. Daily sales in KFC's branches can be 10 times their usual take on Christmas Day.

Mexico

Legend has it that a poor Mexican girl known as Pepita, embarrassed to have nothing else to give, picked a small bunch of weeds to present at a nativity scene. After she placed her humble bouquet down, it burst into a bright flower with five petal-like leaves representing the Star of David.

The poinsettia was from then on always associated with Christmas. 34 million poinsettia are now sold annually the world over.

Netherlands

Known in Holland as Sinterklaas, St. Nicholas was believed to ride a white horse. Dutch children historically left in their shoe a carrot for Sinterklaas's horse, hoping it would be exchanged for a small present.

The Dutch tradition of leaving spiced biscuits for Sinterklaas and a carrot for his trusty steed soon spread around the world. Santa Claus and Rudolf have been the beneficiaries of millions of glasses of milk, sherry or wine and plates of biscuits, cookies and carrots.

Philippines

The city of San Fernando in the Philippines is known as the Christmas capital of the country thanks to its splendid Kapampangan (Giant Lantern Festival).

The *parol*, a beautiful star-shaped lantern crafted from bamboo and paper, has become the iconic image of the Filipino Christmas. At the annual Kapampangan, the stars can reach up to 12 metres (40 feet) in diameter.

Poland

The meat-free Polish Christmas Eve supper *Wigilia* traditionally includes 12 dishes to represent Jesus's 12 disciples. The feast begins after the appearance of the first star.

Sweden

You'll find straw Yule goats decorated with a red ribbon in most Swedish households at Christmas time. As the iconic symbol of Christmas in Sweden, the Yule goat hails from Norse mythology and the idea that the god Thor was pulled across the night sky by two goats.

A modern day Swedish tradition has evolved that includes burning down the large straw Yule goats that are erected in town squares.

Ukraine

Preparations for a traditional Ukrainian *Sviata Vecheria* (Holy Supper) on Christmas Eve:

1. Use two tablecloths, one for the family and one for the ancestors.

2. Place hay under the table to remember Christ was born in a manger in Bethlehem.

3. Decorate the house with sheaves of wheat to bring protection for the coming year.

Venezuela

In Caracas, the capital of Venezuela, local revellers rollerskate to early morning Christmas mass.

Skating to mass has become so popular that the roads now close throughout the city to enable families to skate together safely.

Saturnalia

Including a sacrifice at the temple, rowdy parties in the cities and private gift giving, Saturnalia was an Ancient Roman festival honouring the god Saturn. The riotous partying took place during the second half of December and continued for centuries from at least 217BC to AD300.

" *During my week the serious is barred: no business allowed. Drinking and being drunk, noise and games of dice, appointing of kings and feasting of slaves, singing naked, clapping ... an occasional ducking of corked faces in icy water – such are the functions over which I preside.* "

LUCIAN OF SAMOSATA
From *Saturnalia*

Sol Invictus (the 'Unconquered Sun' God) was declared an official Roman cult by the Roman Emperor Aurelian on 25 December AD274.

Around AD350 Pope Julius I announced that Jesus was born on 25 December. Christmas was officially ON.

"Christmas is joy, religious joy, and an inner joy of light and peace."

POPE FRANCIS

Christmas in Anglo Saxon England started on Christmas Eve and lasted until 2 February – Candlemas Day.

While a whole month of Christmas sounds terrific, most of it would be spent fasting. So, not really Christmas as we know it, at all!

St. Francis of Assisi is credited with using a cave to create the first nativity scene in the small Italian town of Greccio in 1223. He invited villagers to see his living crib, with hay, an ass, ox and a manger, while he preached about the 'Babe of Bethlehem'. (Presumably Jesus, not Mary.)

What do the Popular Colours of Christmas Represent?

Red: Christ's blood

Green: life and rebirth

Gold: light, royalty and wealth

Christmas Calendar

Stir-up Sunday, last Sunday before Advent: stir the Christmas pudding

Advent Sunday: the start of the traditional period of contemplation and fasting before Christmas

St. Nicholas Day, 6 December: historically when children wrote to Father Christmas

Christmas Eve, 24 December: the last day of the advent fast

Christmas Day, 25 December: the first of the Twelve Days of Christmas

Holy Innocents Day, 28 December: the commemoration of Herod's slaughter of the innocents

Twelfth Night, 5 January: the last and final day of Christmas

Epiphany, 6 January: celebration of the visit of the wise men. Time to take the decorations down

Candlemas Day, 2 February: the commemoration of Mary's purification at the temple. Until Victorian times this was when Christmas decorations were removed

Before King Edward VII popularized eating turkey for Christmas in the early 20th century, various different meats were enjoyed during historic Christmas feasts, including:

Goose

Collops of bacon

Venison

Peacock

Roast beef

Boar's head

"Pick a berry off the mistletoe
For every kiss that's given
When the berries are all gone
There's an end to kissing."

medieval rhyme

Five Mistletoe Facts (ish)

1. As druids were said to use a golden sickle to cut mistletoe for sacrificial purposes, mistletoe has long been associated with paganism and banned from churches.

2. According to Norse mythology the mistletoe berries represent the goddess Freya's tears after her son was killed with an arrow made of mistletoe wood.

3. Mistletoe came to symbolize love and was strung up as part of a Christmas 'kissing bough'.

4. Cliff Richard's version of 'Mistletoe and Wine' became the biggest selling single of 1988.

5. York Minster, a cathedral in England, enjoyed an old tradition whereby mistletoe was hung upon the high altar and the local criminals pardoned.

"*The earth has grown old with its burden of care, but at Christmas it always is young, the heart of the jewel burns lustrous and fair, and its soul full of music breaks the air, when the song of angels is sung.*"

PHILLIPS BROOKS
From *'The Voice Of The Christ Child'*

A charming Middle Ages tradition saw the singing of lullaby carols that depicted the mother Mary singing to her baby son. Rather terrifyingly, in some, the baby Jesus would reply to his mother and say, 'Quiet! I am trying to sleep,' or 'Don't get too attached I'm going to be crucified before long.'

" *This maiden hight Mary,*
she was full mild,
She knelt before her own dear child.
She lulled, she lapped,
She rolled, she wrapped,
She wept, without a nay;
She rolled him, she dressed him,
She lissed him, she blessed him,
She sang, 'Dear son, lullay.' "

15th-century lullaby carol

Holly and Ivy

- Evergreens, with their magical ability to keep their colour as other trees shed their leaves, have long been associated with midwinter and Christmas festivals.

- Holly and ivy were particularly treasured and placed over mantels and fireplaces as decorations.

- The Church developed the legend that Christ's cross was made from holly wood and the berries were stained red by Jesus's blood.

- The holly, with its strong pricking leaves represents masculinity, and the ivy femininity.

The holly and the ivy,
When they are both full grown,
Of all the trees that are in the wood,
The holly bears the crown.
The rising of the sun
And the running of the deer,
The playing of the merry organ,
Sweet singing in the choir.

From 'The Holly and the Ivy'
an English folk carol

In 1522 Henry VIII wrote a Christmas carol, 'Green Groweth the Holly'. It would be the equivalent of The Queen of England writing a #1 Christmas song today.

Green groweth the holly,
So doth the ivy.
Though winter blasts blow never
so high,
Green groweth the holly.

HENRY VIII
From 'Green Groweth the Holly'

Legend insists that the first Christmas tree was cut down in the 16th century by Martin Luther, who brought it home and decorated it with candles to imitate 'the starry skies of Bethlehem that Holy Night.'

In 1642 the Puritan English Parliament banned the celebration of Christmas, insisting instead that the day should be spent fasting. No wonder the Puritan Christmas saboteurs were booted out, and Charles II and Christmas were restored in 1660.

Diarist John Evelyn describes Christmas under Christmas-hating Cromwell in 1657.

" I went to London with my wife, to celebrate Christmas-day ... in Exeter Chapel ... the chapel was surrounded with soldiers and all the communicants and assembly surprised and kept prisoners by them, some in the house, others carried away. ... When I came before them, they took my name and abode, examined me why, contrary to the ordinance made, that none should any longer observe the superstitious time of the Nativity."

From 1658–1681 Christmas was officially outlawed in Boston, America. The fine for exhibiting the Christmas spirit was five shillings.

"On one side was a table occupied by some chattering girls, cutting up silk and gold paper; and on the other were tressels and trays, bending under the weight of brawn and cold pies, where riotous boys were holding high revel; the whole completed by a roaring Christmas fire, which seemed determined to be heard, in spite of all the noise of the others."

JANE AUSTEN
From *Persuasion*

"At Christmas, play and make good cheer, for Christmas comes but once a year."

THOMAS TUSSER

The American Who Wrote Christmas

Washington Irving, a wildly successful American man of letters, travelled to England and recorded his experience of an old English Christmas for his 1819 Sketchbook.

Some Christmas cynics claim he made up the whole of this stay with a family called 'Bracebridges'. Whether 100 percent accurate or not, Irving painted a wonderful picture of Christmas in an old English manor house, replete with blistering Yule log, carol singers, mince pies, parlour-maids beneath the mistletoe and hearty Christmas cheer.

"Christmas is a season for kindling the fire for hospitality in the hall, the genial flame of charity in the heart."

WASHINGTON IRVING

"The old halls of castles and manor houses resounded with the harp and the Christmas carol, and their ample boards groaned under the weight of hospitality. Even the poorest cottage welcomed the festive season with green decorations of bay and holly."

WASHINGTON IRVING
From *Old Christmas*

"And when they went away, leaving comfort behind, I think there were not in all the city four merrier people than the hungry little girls who gave away their breakfasts and contented themselves with bread and milk on Christmas morning."

LOUISA M. ALCOTT
From *Little Women*

Posting Christmas Greetings

- Sir Henry Cole, a Victorian businessman commissioned artist John Callcott Horsley to design the first Christmas card in 1843. It shows a happy family enjoying Christmas and kindly souls caring for the poor. Interestingly the children are all enjoying a lovely glass of wine.

- By 1846, 1,000 of these cards had been printed and sold.

- It is estimated that one billion Christmas cards are now sold in the UK every year and two billion are sent around America.

" *To cherish peace and goodwill,
to be plenteous in mercy, is to
have the real spirit of Christmas.*"

CALVIN COOLIDGE

Christmas supremo Charles Dickens originally wrote a political tract about the poor, which was rejected by his publisher for being too dull. Distraught, Dickens walked around London wondering how better he could convey the plight of Victorian paupers. And in a flash, the whole story of *A Christmas Carol* came to him.

Published in 1843, *A Christmas Carol* tells of a miser Ebenezer Scrooge who is turned into a kinder man by the ghosts of Christmas Past, Present and Yet to Come.

" I will honour Christmas in my heart, and try to keep it all the year. I will live in the Past, the Present, and the Future. The Spirits of all Three shall strive within me. I will not shut out the lessons that they teach!"

CHARLES DICKENS
Ebenezer Scrooge in *A Christmas Carol*

"In half a minute Mrs Cratchit entered – flushed by smiling proudly – with the pudding, like a speckled cannon-ball, so hard and firm, blazing in half of half-a-quartern of ignited brandy, and bedight with Christmas holly stuck into the top. Oh, a wonderful pudding! Bob Cratchit said."

CHARLES DICKENS
From *A Christmas Carol*

" God bless us. Every one!"

CHARLES DICKENS
Tiny Tim in *A Christmas Carol*

"There never was such a goose. Bob said he didn't believe there ever was such a goose cooked. Its tenderness and flavour, size and cheapness, were the themes of universal admiration. Eked out by apple sauce and mashed potatoes, it was a sufficient dinner for the whole family; indeed, as Mrs Cratchit said with great delight (surveying one small atom of a bone upon the dish), they hadn't ate it all at last!"

CHARLES DICKENS
From *A Christmas Carol*

Brilliant Christmas Inventions

1. Christmas crackers: invented by sweet manufacturer Tom Smith in the 1840s, now over 150 million crackers are pulled each Christmas in Britain.

2. Advent calendars: Gerhard Lang is considered the first commercial maker of advent calendars in Germany in the 1900s.

3. Tinsel: invented in Nuremburg in 1610, tinsel was originally coated in real silver.

4. Baubles: first made by Hans Greiner in Germany in the 16th century.

Christmas Myth Busting #1

Prince Albert didn't bring the Christmas tree over from Germany to Victorian England.

An earlier German-born monarch, Queen Charlotte of Mecklenburg-Strelitz, the wife of George III, is believed to have introduced the Christmas tree to England in around 1800.

" *In the middle of the room stood an immense tub with a yew tree placed in it, from the branches of which hung bunches of sweetmeats, almonds, and raisins in papers, fruits and toys, most tastefully arranged, and the whole illuminated by small wax candles. After the company had walked around and admired the tree, each child obtained a portion of the sweets which it bore together with a toy and then all returned home, quite delighted.* "

EDWARD HOLT

From *The Public and Domestic Life of George III*

Christmas Trees Take Over Victorian Yuletide

Prince Albert and Queen Victoria can take credit for introducing a domestic German tradition to the whole of the western world.

It's all thanks to an image in the 1848 *Illustrated London News* of the royal family surrounding a Christmas tree at Windsor Castle. Now looking distinctly modest, the small Christmas tree, lovingly decorated with candles and gifts, presented such a scene of Christmas joy that the tradition spread from royal palaces to the most humble of abodes.

German immigrants carried the custom of Christmas trees to America and, fittingly, tree decoration is recorded from 1747 in Bethlehem, Pennsylvania.

It's thanks to American President Grover Cleveland, who decorated the tree at the White House with electric lights in 1895, that the other famous Christmas tradition, of unknotting last year's lights, was born.

" Fine old Christmas, with the snowy hair and ruddy face, had done his duty that year in the noblest fashion, and had set off his rich gifts of warmth and colour with all the heightening contrast of frost and snow."

GEORGE ELIOT
From *The Mill on the Floss*

Christmas was declared a federal holiday on 26 June 1870 by President Ulysses S. Grant.

" Christmas is not a time, nor a season, but a state of mind."

CALVIN COOLIDGE

Footballs were kicked, rather than bombs dropped, during an unofficial series of truces in the trenches during World War One. The first Christmas truce began on Christmas Eve 1914 when French, German and British soldiers crossed trenches to share Christmas greetings and the fabled game of football.

Festival of Nine Lessons and Carols

For the angelic voice of Christmas, tune into the UK's BBC Radio Four on Christmas Eve and enjoy the Festival of Nine Lessons and Carols from King's College, Cambridge.

Now broadcast to over 30 million listeners, the festival had its beginnings after the First World War. Eric Milner-White, dean of the college was so shattered by what he experienced as army padre on the Western Front that on his return to Cambridge he wanted to revive Christmas worship.

First broadcast in 1928, the service follows the same format every year. It famously opens with a young solo chorister singing 'Once in Royal David's City'. None of the 16 choristers know who will be the soloist until the news is read out on the hour before the broadcast. The choir's director then nods to the chosen boy and the crystal notes of 'Once in Royal...' mark, for many, the official start to Christmas.

World Changing Events that Happened on Christmas Day

800 – Charlemagne was crowned Emperor by Pope Leo III in Rome.

1066 – William the Conqueror was crowned in Westminster Abbey after his triumph at the Battle of Hastings.

1968 – Apollo 8 broadcast live from its journey around the moon – at the time, the transmission was the most watched programme ever.

1989 – Communist Romanian dictator Nicolae Ceaușescu and his wife Elena were tried and executed.

The Birth of Santa Claus

Peer through the mists of cold, dark, pagan Northern Europe and you will see the tall, bearded, cloaked figure of the Norse god Woden (or Odin).

Woden travelled the midnight sky by sleigh and was celebrated during the midwinter feast of Yule.

Some folklorists say it is from Woden that the idea comes of Santa Claus hailing from the North Pole – or at least somewhere far north and jolly cold.

Postal Addresses of Father Christmas:

- Santa's Grotto, Reindeerland, XM4 5HQ
- 325 S. Santa Claus Lane, North Pole, Alaska 99705
- 96930, Arctic Circle, Finland
- North Pole, HOH OHO, Canada

"For it is in giving that we receive."

FRANCIS OF ASSISI

St. Nicholas the First Gift-Giver

Born in AD270, Nicholas became Bishop of Myra. A legend evolved around his kindliness, particularly to an impoverished widower with three beautiful daughters and no money for a dowry.

The story goes that he tossed a bag of gold coins down the chimney, which landed in a stocking that was hanging on the fireplace. When the widower spotted him, Nicholas made him promise not to tell anyone. The widower was obviously terrible at keeping secrets and a Christmas hero was born.

The festive tradition of gift giving on St. Nicholas Day, 6 December, eventually melded with the idea of a kindly father figure sharing presents at Christmas time.

" *Down the chimney St. Nicholas came with a bound.*
He was dressed all in fur, from his head to his foot.
And his clothes were all tarnished with ashes and soot."

CLEMENT CLARKE MOORE
From *A Visit from St. Nicholas*

Originally St. Nicholas punished naughty children as well as rewarding good ones. In Germany he is said to carry a black book recording their misdeeds and is accompanied by a hobgoblin, Krampus, Ruprecht or Hans Scruff, who whips those who deserve it.

"But where I found the children naughty,
In manners rude, in temper haughty,
Thankless to parents, liars, swearers,
Boxers, or cheats, or base tale-bearers,

I left a long, black, birchen rod,
Such as the dread command of God
Directs a Parent's hand to use
When virtue's path his sons refuse."

CLEMENT CLARKE MOORE
From *Old Santeclaus*

" Now, Dasher! now, Dancer! now Prancer and Vixen!
On, Comet! on, Cupid! on, Donner and Blitzen!
To the top of the porch! to the top of the wall!
Now dash away! dash away! dash away all!"

CLEMENT CLARKE MOORE
From *A Visit from St. Nicholas*

By the Tudor period, the pagan God Woden / Odin and St. Nicholas had merged into the figure of Old Man Christmas who we would recognize today as Father Christmas. Wearing a hat and long cloak, sometimes green, sometimes red, sometimes brown (what a relief that didn't catch on), Old Man Christmas wore a substantial beard and was most concerned with bringing good cheer.

*" Love is the moral of Christmas ...
What are gifts but the proof and
signs of love?"*

Harper's Magazine

Quite when Father Christmas began to speak will remain a deep mystery but all authorities agree that 'HO! HO! HO!' is a unique Santa greeting.

Different Names for Santa Claus

America: Santa Claus

Britain: Father Christmas

Netherlands: Sinterklaas

Finland: Joulupukki

France: Père Nöel

Gaelic: Nollaig

Germany: Weihnachtsmann

Japan: Santa-San (Mr Santa)

Norway: Julenissen

Portugal: Pai Natal

Russia: Ded Moroz

*"He had a broad face and
a little round belly
That shook when he laughed,
like a bowl full of jelly.
He was chubby and plump,
a right jolly old elf."*

CLEMENT CLARKE MOORE
From *A Visit from St. Nicholas*

Slavic pagan tradition sees Ded Moroz (Grandfather Frost) as the chief winter gift-giver. Dressed in a rather fetching blue fur robe, Ded Moroz is an altogether more imposing figure than Santa. He is accompanied by Snegurochka, his snow maiden granddaughter and helper.

Christmas as a Feminist Affair

For certain sections of Germanic Europe, folklore held it was female figures that roamed the countryside punishing naughty children and rewarding the good.

In Bavaria and Austria the figure of Christmas dread was known as Bertha, Holda or Perchta. Particularly interested in punishing women and girls who hadn't finished their spinning, Bertha, Holda or Perchta were reputed to carry naughty children into the woods and even to stuff them as dolls. Good children on the other hand could expect a present.

Whether Santa has a wife is hotly debated. Sometimes known as Mary Christmas, Mrs Claus first appeared in 'A Christmas Legend', a short story published in 1849.

Italy has a kind female Christmas gift-giver in the form of La Befana (meaning Epiphany). Legend has it that she arrived too late in Bethlehem to worship the baby Jesus so was condemned to wander the earth giving gifts to children. She visits houses, sings and dances to bring families good luck and leaves sweets, oranges and toys in the children's stockings.

Home is where the heart is (especially at Christmas time).

Keen to shrug off links to England after the War of Independence, Americans embraced the Dutch immigrants personification of Christmas, Sinterklaas (St. Nicholas).

Sinterklaas had by the 19th century become, in all his red and white glory, Santa Claus.

"Old Santeclaus with much delight
His reindeer drives this frosty night,
O'er chimney-tops, and tracks of snow,
To bring his yearly gifts to you."

CLEMENT CLARKE MOORE
From *Old Santeclaus*

Who Has Played Santa Claus on the Big Screen?

1. Edmund Gwenn, *Miracle on 34th Street*, 1947

2. David Huddleston, *Santa Claus: The Movie*, 1985

3. Tim Allen, *The Santa Clause*, 1994

4. Richard Attenborough, *Miracle on 34th Street*, 1994

5. Ed Asner, *Elf*, 2003

6. Tom Hanks (voice), *The Polar Express*, 2004

Santa's sleigh would have to travel 2,340,000 mph if he were to reach every home on Christmas Eve. No problem: **he's magic**.

What Does Santa Leave for Naughty Children?

America: Coal

Hungary: A birch stick to be whipped with

Iceland: Potatoes

Christmas Myth Busting #2

Coca-Cola did not invent Santa Claus's clothes

Urban myth insists that Santa's signature red and white outfit was designed as a marketing tool by Coca-Cola. In fact, Santa Claus had been depicted in red and white get up for a good century before Coca-Cola's graphic designers were sharpening their crayons.

When Santa's Clothes Became Red and White

- Santa Claus is shown wearing red in his sleigh in an illustration to accompany the 1821 book *A New-Year's Present, To The Little Ones From Five to Twelve*.

- Most famously, Thomas Nast, a German born American illustrator, depicted 'Merry old Santa Claus' as a white bearded, rosy-cheeked fellow for *Harper's Weekly*.

- By 1902, Santa Claus in mandatory red and white suit can be seen clambering in through a window on the front cover of *Puck* magazine.

Coca-Cola certainly helped catapult the image of Santa around the world, when they commissioned illustrator Haddon Sundblom to design a Coca-Cola-drinking Santa.

Sundblom's fat and friendly creation debuted in 1931 and Coca-Cola's global reach has cemented Santa's image for now. But who knows how the Christmas character will develop in the following centuries.

J.R. Roberts department store in East London opened the first Santa's grotto in 1888.

In some parts of Europe it was the baby Jesus who was believed to have delivered presents. In Austria and Germany the present giver was a golden-haired, bewinged baby who represents Jesus as the *Christkind* (Christ Child).

In modern day Czech Republic there are efforts to elbow out 'modern' Santa Claus and bring back the older tradition of the *Ježíšek* – the baby Jesus present giver.

In 2016, the most popular pantomimes across the UK in terms of attendance figures were:

1. *Cinderella* (652,748 tickets sold)

2. *Dick Whittington* (466,597 tickets sold)

3. *Jack and the Beanstalk* (392,256 tickets sold)

4. *Aladdin* (389,256 tickets sold)

5. *Beauty and the Beast* (339,400 tickets sold)

6. *Snow White* (314,591 tickets sold)

7. *Peter Pan* (206,868 tickets sold)

8. Other (170,911 tickets sold)

Christmas Feasts

Until the 1950s most British households had goose or beef for Christmas Day. Nowadays however, a traditional English Christmas roast dinner consists of...

Turkey

Stuffing

Pigs in blankets

Chestnuts

Roast potatoes

Roast Parsnips

Brussels Sprouts

Red cabbage

Carrots

Cranberry Sauce

Bread Sauce

Gravy

Turkey with all the trimmings weighs in at approximately 2,000 calories. With chocolate from the stocking, Champagne breakfast, sherry and nibbles, Christmas pudding and then supper, it's estimated that people can consume over 5,000 calories on Christmas Day.

Is that all?

Figgy Pudding Recipe

Take almaundes blanched, grynde hem and draw hem up with water and wyne: quarter fygur, hole raisouns. Cast perto powdour gyngur and hony clarified, seeth it well & salt it, and serue forth.

**THE MASTER COOKS OF
KING RICHARD II**
From *The Forme of Cury*

From the medieval frumenty, a sloppy sort of fig pudding, to the Georgian plum pudding, Christmas pudding arrived in all its spherical splendour in the Victorian period.

Rich in raisins, currants, brandy, and the all important beef suet, Christmas pudding is the traditional way to finish off Christmas dinner.

Serve Christmas pudding flaming with brandy and lashings of brandy butter / double cream / custard / ice cream... (after all it is Christmas).

Three Things to Find in a Christmas Pudding:

1. Silver coin: wealth

2. Ring: marriage

3. Thimble: spinsterhood

Minced Meat to Mince Pies

- Originally minced pies contained a total of 13 ingredients representing Christ and his Apostles.

- Gervase Markham's 1615 recipe book included an entire leg of mutton for the minced pie recipe.

- By 1747 in Hannah Glasse's *Art of Cookery* book, minced pies were sweet (phew!).

- Around 370 million mince pies are sold over the Christmas period in the UK.

- The average Briton eats 27 mince pies a year (is that all?).

" Leaving my wife desirous to sleep, having sat up til four in the morning seeing her mayds make mince-pies."

SAMUEL PEPYS

Once an enormous log that would be cut on Christmas Eve and burnt throughout Christmas until Twelfth Night, the Yule log is now a gooey chocolate confection. Traditionally made with a genoise sponge and lathered in chocolate ganache, the Yule log is decorated with sprigs of holly and sometimes dusted with icing to resemble snow. So much tastier than its wooden original.

Traditionally Christmas festivities finished on the old Twelfth Night, 5 January, when a rich and crumbly fruit cake would be made. Baked inside the cake were a dried bean and pea and whoever found them would be named King and Queen of the Revels.

On the twelfth day of Christmas
My true love sent to me
Twelve fiddlers fiddling,
Eleven ladies dancing,
Ten pipers piping,
Nine drummers drumming,
Eight maids a-milking,
Seven swans a-swimming,
Six geese a-laying,
Five gold rings,
Four colly birds,
Three French hens,
Two turtle doves, and
A partridge in a pear tree.

From 'The Twelve Days of Christmas'
an English Christmas carol

154

Christmas is a time for giving.

Well I Never Knew That About Christmas...

- Taylor Swift grew up on a Christmas tree farm in Pennsylvania.

- English sea captain William Mynors named Christmas Island while sailing past it on 25 December 1643.

- Research by Royal Mail reveals that Britain has over 3,000 Christmas themed street names, from Tinsel Lane in Nuneaton to Reindeer Close in East London.

Most Snowmen Built in One Hour

Total: 2,036

Participants: 1,406

When: 2015

Where: Japan

Christmas Names for Girls

Carol

Joy

Angel

Bell

Holly

Gloria

Mary

Natalie

Christmas Names for Boys

Noel

Nicholas

Rudolf

Joseph

Gabriel

Emmanuel

Goose Feathers

Due to major deforestation in late 19th-century Germany, artificial Christmas trees were developed.
The first artificial Christmas tree was created out of goose feathers that were dyed green.

Santa's Reindeer

On Christmas Eve, Santa's sleigh is pulled through the night sky by nine flying reindeer:

Dasher

Dancer

Prancer

Vixen

Comet

Cupid

Donner

Blitzen

Rudolph

The Most Listened to Christmas Songs Globally:

1. 'All I Want for Christmas is You', Mariah Carey

2. 'It's Beginning to Look a Lot Like Christmas', Michael Bublé

3. 'Christmas Lights', Coldplay

4. 'Last Christmas', Wham!

5. 'Do You Hear What I Hear?', Bing Crosby

6. 'Have Yourself a Merry Little Christmas', Sam Smith

7. 'I'll Be Home', Meghan Trainor

8. 'Driving Home for Christmas', The Mington Winters

9. 'Winter Wonderland / Don't Worry Be Happy', Pentatonix ft. Tori Kelly

10. 'One More Sleep', Leona Lewis

SPOTIFY USA

Hey, Big Spender

- £1.6 billion was spent on Christmas in the UK in 2018.

- The average American spent roughly $700 on Christmas gifts and goodies in 2018.

- 83 square km of wrapping paper is sold in the UK every Christmas.

- A typical UK household spends an extra £500 in December.

Christmas with The Queen at Sandringham

Tradition dictates that the Royal Family bestow on each other joke presents. Such rib-tickling offerings include a shower cap from Prince Harry to his Grandmother adorned with the words, 'Ain't life a b**ch!'. Kate Middleton is said to have given Prince Harry, when single, A 'Grow Your Own Girlfriend kit'. It obviously worked, as last year Meghan Markle presented The Queen with a singing hamster toy, which was said to have had everyone in hysterics.

The BBC's *Songs of Praise* Revealed Britain's Favourite Carols

Hark! The Herald Angels Sing

In the Bleak Midwinter

It Came Upon a Midnight Clear

Joy to the World

O Come All Ye Faithful

O Come, O Come Emmanuel

O Holy Night

O Little Town of Bethlehem

Once in Royal David's City

Silent Night

Christmas Tree Gifts

Since 1947, the city of Oslo has given a Christmas tree to Britain as thanks for its support during World War Two. The magnificent Norwegian Spruce is displayed in Trafalgar Square.

Since 1971, the people of Nova Scotia have given a large Christmas tree to the City of Boston to thank it for its help during the 1917 Halifax explosion.

Popular Christmas Tree Varieties

Douglas Fir

Balsam Fir

Fraser Fir

Canaan Fir

Scots Pine

White Pine

White Spruce

Norwegian Spruce

Blue Spruce

Today, there are approximately 25–30 million real Christmas trees sold annually in America.

There are currently 350 million Christmas trees growing on American tree farms.

Well I Never Knew That About Christmas...

- The most searched Christmas hashtags on Instagram are: #Sleigh, #ChristmasSpirit and #ChristmasMagic.

- The bestselling Christmas single ever is Bing Crosby's 'White Christmas' shifting over 50 million copies since 1942.

- The longest paper chain measures 779.21 m (2,556 ft 5.5 in) long and was achieved by Julie McKinney (USA) in 2014.

The first royal Christmas Message was broadcast by radio in 1932 by King George V and was listened to by 20 million people.

HM The Queen has broadcast the *Royal Christmas Message* every year (apart from 1969) since 1952. Over six million people tuned in to watch the broadcast in 2018.

Three Easy Christmas Crafts

1. Fill a jar with Maltesers and label it 'Reindeer Poo'.

2. Pin a cork to the base of a pinecone, paint the tips of the pinecone green for a perfect mini Christmas tree.

3. Paint dried pasta bows in gold glitter and tie with ribbon for a miniature Christmas decoration.

The NORAD (North American Aerospace Defense Command) Santa Tracker has 1.8 million followers on its Facebook page. The programme, which follows Santa's progress around the globe from the North Pole, has existed since 1955.

The Royal Family's Guide to Christmas

Tom Smith Crackers:

Tom Smith Crackers, based in Ystrad Mynach in Wales has been supplying the Royal Household with bespoke Christmas crackers since 1906.

Keep Christmas Cards Brief:

Though The Queen and The Duke of Edinburgh send out around 750 Christmas cards, they are simply signed 'Elizabeth R' and 'Philip' – no round robin letters for them.

Christmas Pudding:

The Queen gives all of her staff, around 1,500 of them, a Christmas pudding. Apparently royal employees receive Tesco's Finest Matured Christmas Pudding.

Best Christmas Cracker Jokes

Q) Who hides in a bakery at Christmas?

A) A mince spy

Q) What do you get if you cross Father Christmas with a duck?

A) A Christmas quacker

Q) What do you get if you swallow Christmas decorations?

A) Tinsillitis

Q) What did one snowman say to the other?

A) Can you smell carrot?

Q) What music do elves listen to?

A) Wrap

Q) Who is Rudolf's favourite singer?

A) Beyon-sleigh

A Not So Merry Christmas...

" December, no longer simply a month, now takes up the whole year."

SENECA

" 'Bah,' said Scrooge, 'Humbug.'
'If I could work my will ... every idiot
who goes about with "Merry Christmas"
on his lips should be boiled with his
own pudding and buried with a stake of
holly through his heart. He should!' "

CHARLES DICKENS
Ebenezer Scrooge in *A Christmas Carol*

"Santa Claus has the right idea – visit people only once a year."

VICTOR BORGE

Alternative Christmas Greetings

Happy Holidays

Season's Greetings

Winter Wishes

Holiday Greetings

"All I want for Christmas is for it to be over."

ANON

We wish you a merry Christmas,
We wish you a merry Christmas,
We wish you a merry Christmas
And a happy New Year.

Glad tidings we bring
To you and your kin;
We wish you a merry Christmas
And a happy New Year!

From 'We Wish You a Merry Christmas'
a traditional English carol

Christmas Fun and Games

- Snapdragon: popular from the 16th century, snapdragon requires brandy to be poured over a shallow dish of raisins, and set aflame. With dimmed lights, partygoers snatch the fruit and put out the flames in their mouth – not for the faint hearted!

- Are you there Moriarty? Two players are blindfolded and kneel down in front of each other. They are handed a rolled up newspaper and the first player shouts, *"Are you there Moriarty?"*. The second player crawls away and replies, *"Yes!"*. The first player attempts to hit the crouching second player with his newspaper. The second player recovers from the paper attack and asks *"Are you there Moriarty?"*. And repeat until either the players or newspaper are destroyed.

The true spirit of Christmas is **love**.

Fa la la la la la la la la.

From 'Deck The Halls'
a traditional Christmas carol

QUOTES ARE TAKEN FROM:

Calvin Coolidge was the 30th President of the United States

Charles Dickens was an English writer and is regarded by many as the greatest novelist of the Victorian era

Christina Rossetti was a 19th-century English poet

Clement Clarke Moore was a 19th-century American writer

Francis of Assisi was a 13th-century Italian saint

George Eliot was a 19th-century English novelist

Henry VIII was King of England, best known for his six marriages

Jane Austen was an English novelist known for her six major novels

John Evelyn was a 17th-century English diarist

Louisa M. Alcott was a 19th-century American novelist, best known for *Little Women*

Lucian of Samosata was a 2nd-century Syrian satirist

Phillips Brooks was a 19th-century American clergyman

Pope Francis has been Pope since 2013

Samuel Pepys was a 17th-century English diarist

Seneca was a Roman Stoic philosopher

Thomas Hardy was a renowned Victorian poet and novelist

Thomas Tusser was a 16th-century English poet

Victor Borge was a Danish-American comedian

Washington Irving was a 19th-century American writer

BIBLIOGRAPHY AND FURTHER READING

Holy Bible, King James Version, 1611

Jane Austen, *Persuasion*, 1817

Margaret Baker, *Discovering Christmas Customs and Folklore*, 1968

Carleton Brown, *Religious Lyrics of the XVth Century*, 1939

Tristram P. Coffin, *The Book of Christmas Folklore*, 1973

Charles Dickens, *A Christmas Carol*, 1843

Mark Forsyth, *A Christmas Cornucopia*, 2016

Edward Holt, *The Public and Domestic Life of George III*, 1820

Jacqueline Simpson, *European Mythology*, 1987

Jane Struthers, *The Book of Christmas*, 2012

USEFUL WEBSITES

www.spotify.com

www.hymnsandcarolsofchristmas.com

www.northpole.com

www.noradsanta.org

Publishing Director Sarah Lavelle
Editor Harriet Webster
Assistant Editor Stacey Cleworth
Words Joanna Gray
Series Designer Emily Lapworth
Design Assistant Christine Geiger
Production Director Vincent Smith
Production Controller Katie Jarvis

Published in 2019 by Quadrille,
an imprint of Hardie Grant
Publishing

Quadrille
52–54 Southwark Street
London SE1 1UN
quadrille.com

The publisher has made every
effort to trace the copyright
holders. We apologize in advance
for any unintentional omissions
and would be pleased to insert the
appropriate acknowledgement in
any subsequent edition.

Cataloguing in Publication Data:
a catalogue record for this book is
available from the British Library.

ISBN 978 1 78713 479 9

Printed in China